The Red Window

Marianne Aweagon Broyles

WEST END PRESS

Poems from *The Red Window* have been published in: *Hellp!, Puerto del Sol, Snowy Egret, Santa Fe Literary Review*, and *Red Ink*.

First edition, September 2008
Paperback 978-0-9816693-1-1

Book and cover design by Nancy Woodard
Cover art by Donovan Henan (Shoshone/Navajo)
Interior art by John Timothy II (Muscogee Creek)
Author and cover photographs by Diane Fields

For book information, see our Web site at www.westendpress.org.

The Red Window is the premier publication in the West End Press New Series, featuring first full-length volumes by emerging and more established poets.

West End Press
PO Box 27334
Albuquerque, NM 87125

Contents

Estate Sale

Even with its good intentions, early afternoon
sun participates in the worst kind of voyeurism,
lending a garish cast on our patch of
working-class neighborhood.
Alongside bargain-hunters congregated
on her front lawn,
I remain an uncomfortable first-time observer—
not really wanting to rifle through
a dead stranger's life like an archaeologist.

Still, I am here, watching and busying
myself while my relatives with flannel
coats, baseball caps, tinted bifocals
blend with their fellow Minnesotans.

Some drink old coffee from Styrofoam cups.
Some sit on a brown and mustard floral sofa
while others examine muffin tins and pots
or *Reader's Digest* condensed books.

Overcome by morbid curiosity, I step
into her home, also on the auction block.
No one is there but me in the heavy quiet
of her Formica kitchen.
There is a sea of photographs tacked on peeling
green and blue wallpaper.
People she loved or who loved her long ago.
School pictures, weddings, proms.
Her living memorial, her wall of honor.

I turn away to go back outside, not wanting to be
in so much loneliness.
The auctioneer looks small through the screen door,
going on and on like an electric saw
while cousin Bernadette walks up to report we're leaving—

there's nothing here worth buying.

Where Myth Becomes a Panther

I let myself go
to old Highway 9
where black panthers are seen
by Oklahomans of all kinds.

Many experts say it is not true—it
may only be a once-captive black leopard
crouching low along the South Canadian River,
making its way through heavy brush as if it owned the world.

But I believe it is a panther, like the old stories,
as black as a wall cloud forming
in the dead of night, with its golden eyes always calculating
what is prey and what is not like a ruthless general.

I believe it is just like Jackson Narcomey told us,
It ran across the highway right in front of my truck and
jumped over the fence of an old Creek allotment.
Then it just disappeared as if it had gone through a hole in the sky.

I know what I saw.

Crossing Lake Eufaula

Hwy 695 near Krebs, Oklahoma

Just when I think I can't take any more
          open plains, we cross Lake Eufaula,
acres and acres of water
in the horizon.

There are lake homes enclosed by pines and boats tied at private docks.
I say *I'd like to live here one day.*
The atmosphere changes to twilight, and the sun has its last show of power
for this day
—white and blinding.

You don't answer right away, so I wait. Then your words
form like the unfolding of an origami crane.

No one said they knew it, but this lake was built on burial mounds
of the Mississippian culture, or maybe the Hopewells,
so I wouldn't do that, you say.

There is a cedar home with a red Volvo parked on gravel drive.
          No signs of the family.
Two fishermen sit by the bridge pilings, wait for bass.

Never pick anything up from here either, you add.
Leave it all here where it belongs.
You wouldn't want to take something like that with you.

The sun now glows orange,
begins to sink
below the chop of Lake Eufaula

that contains our silence like rain.

Thirteen

My mother wanted short hair so much it didn't stop her
even though she says her father wept
when she went to the beauty shop in downtown Okmulgee
to have her braids cut off.

But she was thirteen and old enough to do
what she wanted with her hair.

Her father asked her to carry the braids home
so he could keep them. He gave her a white tie box
before she walked out the door.

I wonder what my mother thought about on the way home.
Did she know it would be so quick, so easy?
Did she know how light it would feel?

When she arrived at the front door, she presented the braids
in the white box to her father. A floral delivery with nothing
to sign to indicate his acceptance.
He walked with them to his makeshift office in the back,
somberly opened the top desk drawer, put in the box,
and closed it like a mausoleum of her girlhood.

Even when she went back
to 1500 South Delaware, back to Okmulgee
from California for the holidays,
she always knew her braids were still
in the same white box
in her father's top desk drawer
as if she might someday change her mind
and ask to have them back.

First Grade School Photograph

It took twenty-five minutes of crying and begging
before I wore my mother down. I awoke ready
for it, anticipating the moment when
she would present that red gingham dress,
with its large, lace-trimmed heart personalized
with my name spelled right—*Marianne*.

My mother brought it in, as I knew she would,
even at seven years old.

After one year, I had already outgrown
the gingham's innocent charm and longed for my
Spanish-colored silk dress—triangles, rectangles,
diamonds crazily pieced together like a Picasso
in Sangria, Olive, Mediterranean Blue, Blood Orange—
so unlike the baby-red gingham with my name on it
as if I didn't know who I was.

And when I finally went out the door that
hard-fought morning, triumphant in my Spanish dress,
I began to let myself slowly fall away,
like weathered tiles,
before I could let my mother return.

Visitation

I awoke to a ruckus of soft
thuds. Then my mother's voice
Cut off the fan.
My father emerged from the living room,
holding a frightened thing with
gray feathers and a slender, forked tail.
He spoke to it softly,
like a parent calming a child.
The scissortail had flown down the chimney.
It must have been like falling into the center
of another earth, trapped by glass and doors.
Yet there it was, smudged with soot,
our Oklahoma state bird,
knowing something had gone very wrong.

We watched its panic-stricken eyes trying to see
through my dad's hands, frantic for open sky.
He carried it to the front porch and let go
and it took flight like it had been
tethered for a long time.
Then, my father went back inside
to make sure the flue was completely shut this time.

Bettie Dunback Does Not Rest Here

For my great-great-grandmother, Bettie Dunback,
who survived the Cherokee removal, also known as
"The Trail of Tears," as a young girl

At Greenleaf Cemetery, in Tahlequah,
within the Cherokee Nation.
Only her bones are here.
I can see where the earth was moved
for her grave—a faint rectangular
seam where grass has grown over a scar
healed for many years.
We leave a hanging basket of striped petunias
by her headstone for our own
who walked The Trail as a girl.
We know the flowers won't stay for long.
They will soon be an offering for the living
or moved from grave to grave.
I don't think Bettie would mind too much.
She's not here beneath this plot marked
by an obelisk engraved with vines
that climb away from this earth.

We remain here to imagine.

Tornado Siren

It traces a circle in the still air with a monotonous drone.
That's the Doppler effect, like a train, my dad says,
the change in loudness and pitch. There's nothing like it.
John says if I'm lucky I'll see a tornado
like the time he saw a white stovepipe
emerge from a wall cloud
across the river. When it met the grocery store,
it turned black as its patchwork of debris
wove itself closer and closer until it
became a knotted thing in the busy, angry funnel.

I don't think I ever want to be that kind of lucky.

It is a good day for it, though, when birds vanish
from a bottle-green sky.
Those who know Oklahoma say it's the still
that's so unsettling.
And when the siren's warning
fills the air,
I only hope to witness
when the tornado dips
—a sewing needle undoing threads
of someone else's life,
leaving my own intact.

Mohawk Horse Breaker

His saddle now an oxygen tank, his ropes now its tubing
across his shoulders, around his neck.
My daddy put me on my first horse when I was six,
Philip tells me. His voice rises in anticipation
as if he hears a tangle of galloping hooves
from an Idaho valley.
His eyes shift focus from me
toward the ceiling
as he reaches for memory.
How do you break them? I ask.
Philip laughs. *You just stay on.*
When I was nine, I was breakin horses
with men who were twenty.
Then his eyes darken over—
stars covered by a bank of storm clouds—
as Philip leaves the moment
and returns where he lies now. He releases a sigh,
the same kind of sigh
exhausted Pintos must have
let go under his craggy weight.
Now, I smile at his lizard boots,
sticking out of crumpled hospital bedding,
indicative of his unbroken will.
I sure do love them horses, he declares,
and closes his eyes so he can
rejoin the world he knew before.

Hanhka

With confidence, you steer a green-flamed monster.
The chain steering wheel might as well be horns
twisting like the old Council Oak.

The 1954 Ford F-100 is older than us, rolling off a Detroit
assembly line two years before my parents' marriage.
Made in the day of Miss Americas and Alfred Hitchcock.

As you whip around a corner near the Tulsa fairgrounds,
a man, shirt unbuttoned, salutes your truck's appearance.
His shirt snaps like a flag in the late afternoon breeze.
I hold onto the door, which doesn't always close.

You strapped in? you ask. When you really know
I don't need to tell you I am.

So I settle into the engine's growl, watch side-panel
green flames running like children in the rearview mirror,
feel the centrifugal force as we take each turn like we're
riding on the wing of a pterodactyl.

Hanhka *is Muscogee for bogeyman or monster.*

Train Intuition

I am wakened by the train
    rolling through town
rolling near
the giant Holiday Inn
filled with a random
smattering of occupants, like me, who lie
in their beds—pins stuck
in a tomato pincushion
    for safekeeping in the night.
Now, some hear the train
and some do not, but it
passes by anyway,
    oblivious to human validation.

Before, I slept through the night train,
conditioning myself to accept its inevitability.
One always flew by Atlanta,
alongside our Emory dormitory.
I'd hear it approach—its
    low-pitched war cry
getting higher and louder,
the vibrations of its wake,
its bright headlight passing
    by half-open windows.

Those first August nights, it would wake us
like a knock on the door.
Nearly a hundred pairs of eyes would
    open and close/open and close/
as it passed us by,
as we stepped in and out
of our nighttime thoughts
that ran like an autumn stream
    in the North Georgia mountains.

American Revolution

*In honor of Po'pay (San Juan Pueblo),
instigator of the Pueblo Revolt, 1680*

Most wouldn't see freedom in a
knotted rope—a different use from tying things
down or securing the defeated.

Each knot represented a day until the revolt.
The runners you sent knew, too, that what could
be counted, what could be seen and held,
could transcend language.

When the last knot was reached
the time arrived. Like night dissolving
for daybreak, human blood not
labeled Spanish or Pueblo melt
in the earth for liberation.
To abandon mines of prosperity,
to walk their land without fear.

Your people slept knowing they'd wake
in a different world.
Tell me, since your statue won't,
where did you wake?

The Londoners

In memory of Oukah-Ulah, Oukanekah, Kettagustah, Tathtiowie, Clogittah, Collanah, and Ounakannowie, who made the voyage to England aboard the Fox with Sir Alexander Cuming on May 4, 1730

What did the seven Cherokee men think
when they arrived in England after a month at sea?
They were living proof of colonial alliance
as they lived their everyday Cherokee lives,
as best they could, in an undertaker's basement.
Onlookers paid to peek at them through windows.
They must have eaten kidney pie and goose paté
on delicate china, finished with a crystal glass of port,
just like their British hosts.

What did they think of their portraits painted with fine oils?
Did they accept different names in quiet resignation
living among an unfamiliar tongue?
Did they feel any more civilized than they did
in their Cherokee towns, smoking a pipe
and telling their children legends of the autumn sky?

Drawing by John Timothy II (Muscogee Creek).

Cheyenne Chief Black Kettle Meets Custer

Along the Washita River, 1868

What did you think that winter day
when you rode, your wife beside you,
to meet the General?

Even though the first time, four years ago
at Sand Creek, the flag of truce meant
nothing to soldiers looking for gold who found
your people in the way?

Now, it is the same predicament.

What did you think that winter day
when you rode, your wife beside you,
to meet the General?

Did the snow hitting your face seem colder,
did the whipping of the white flag seem louder?

Was the last vision of this earth you loved
the long, black barrel of the General's gun?

The Son of God

At the bus stop, he approaches us
to deliver his message
on a poster with worn corners.
He yells at us through the glass
in his Caribbean dialect
while pounding his staff
—festooned with bottle caps and plastic jewels—
onto the dirty sidewalk.
He shakes the sign in perfect
synchronicity with his staff as if he
is a leader of a marching band.

the seattle police are liars.
they are all satan. the church is full of liars.
i am the son of god.

The remaining red paint letters are blocked by the bus door
but he sees me through the window, leaning to read the rest
of his message, and fixates on my eyes. His blaze with fanaticism.
I look away quickly, then back, thinking it might be safe.
But it isn't.

Finally, the driver reaches for the handle
to pull the doors shut with a gasp. As we lurch away
from the curb, I join the others in the conspiracy
of pretending he's not really there, as if we're
all embarrassed for him.

Still, I turn and watch the son of god back away from our bus
and approach people leaving a Starbucks with backpacks or
briefcases. They hold their coffees tightly as he searches
for the one who may be his prodigal.

Meeting the Code Talker

He wears traditional warrior colors for the presentation
of the colors ceremony to honor our Navajo code talkers.

> *(A gold shirt for corn pollen,*
> *brown pants for Mother Earth.)*

He sits silently
beside his wife
on the bench in Cathedral Park.
Both his hands firmly cover the handle
of his cane as if he is the top of a
wild onion adhered in the red earth.

John says *let's thank this man for what he has done for our country*
as we touch palms lightly.

Although he is old now, and his remaining years
could be counted like loose pocket change,
I imagine him young, clutching a radio,
the echo of artillery fire as discernible as a bell.
His body tight as the finest weaving.

Somewhere in Arizona, in that moment,
did his mother pause to touch the back
of an empty chair at the table
before getting dinner off the stove?

84th Indian Market

He does not ask for money.
He does not make eye contact
even though people turn to look back
as they pass.
He has made his space on the
sidewalk, facing an intersection
off the plaza.
He sits, cross-legged, before random
items he has spread that look
like candies fallen from a piñata.
I can't help but survey what he
has—Bazooka bubblegum, loose
change, scraps of paper with things
written on them, a book of matches,
a bottle of water with a torn label.
He has lit a thick bundle of sage and
props it on an ashtray.
Despite
the crush of people
with their bags,
plates of fry bread, their Diet Cokes,
their purses, their wallets,
he seems almost prayerful.
He remains so still and quiet he could
be statuary in bronze or granite
beside a plate engraved with his name,
his story, his significance.
But he is not. He is here, in his own world.

No one wants to stop and ask.

Family History

My mother calls you a runner,
like her father, her brothers.
She recounts, for my benefit,
her father's visits to other women.
A child is a good cover,
she says in distant thought.

Tonight, in the family kitchen, you ask me
why I had to ruin
our relationship with my
insistence, determination.
I hate you for it, you announce.

We sit together,
wondering who will get up
and leave first.

I think of my yellow tomcat, Diogenes,
who is, somewhere, on the hunt.
Now I can almost see him,
crouching in the brush,
waiting for a small bird
he will overpower
and carry tenderly home to me.

He'll drop its delicate
life on my doorstep,
only to show his love.

Aunt Pearl

She was not all that far from Sallisaw,
right across the river in Fort Smith.
My grandfather asked my mother to call her *Aunt*
even though she was really
his first of three wives
(as if this would help a thirteen-year-old girl
whose mother, his second wife, had died).

When he crossed
the threshold of her screen door
he'd always call *Pearl! Pearl! It's Watie!*
My mother always trailed behind him,
like she was told.
Aunt Pearl didn't see well anymore
and kept a loaded revolver in her nightstand
even though she was a Pentecostal.
All good Christians should defend
their homes the best they know how.

My mother would wait in the kitchen
during their visits. She'd drink a Coke
and study Aunt Pearl's world
of canned spiced peaches in mason jars,
pickled beets, a *Reader's Digest* tented
on the old wooden table, the smell
of linen on the clothesline
just beyond the open window.

She still says she liked Aunt Pearl—
a good woman who punctuated her father's life,
like her own mother did.
The same way wooden clothespins
keep laundry far enough apart to dry completely
without falling from the line.

Tear Dress

It is black, trimmed in red satin
for a granddaughter
of the Wolf Clan.
The pattern is so precise,
diamonds near the hem with
straight lines, made so by
patience and
modern convenience.

When my Cherokee ancestors were
on The Trail, the cavalry took
away the women's scissors.

They found other ways.

Like tearing
strips of calico
to make their dresses when
soldier's footsteps
faded with their pipe
smoke and their talking
dwindled to a word
here and there—
an intermittent raindrop *ping*
that hit a tin bucket beneath
the rooftop leak.

Like this,
the sound of an old Cherokee woman
ripping cloth for a tear dress is a
bell in the air—
its own thunderclap,
its own small joy amid destruction.

Accident

My mother and my uncle drove along Colton Avenue,
lined with royal palms, a long way from Wichita.
They weren't expecting a drunken man to step
in their path. A man looking down, not forward, not
toward oncoming traffic. His hands loosely
around what smelled like bourbon—destined to become
my uncle's drink.
Just seconds before, they were laughing, my mother
trying to hold onto her strawberry milkshake.

Then the man intersected their lives.

They couldn't stop in time even
at a moderate cruise. The car was
in its momentum—an American-made
cantering steel horse.

With a thud, the man rolled across
their hood, in slow motion, a grotesque
ballet. His body seemed like he had
no bones as he hit the Buick's insignia
that rose from the hood like an early moon
before he met pavement again.

My mother and uncle leapt from the car—
asked him if he was hurt. His bottle was broken, like
a heart—the liquor flooded out—its smell an
intruder in the clean night air,
the scent of orange groves never far away.

Then he looked up at my mother in her white
sundress, her tanned skin, her black hair.
His hand still around the neck of his
bottle. His eyes closed for a moment,
then opened again.

She leaned over, looked into his face
as he asked,
Are you an angel?

Shell Shakers (Never Stop Dancing)

I've already worn their shells, heard stories of turtles
gathered from alongside ponds, highways, backyards.
How their insides are scooped out,
cleaned, dried, then their emptiness filled with stones or cherry pits

so they can be used to shake as we move around the stomp ground's fire
and form a string of clay with Indians falling off and adding on
like a restrung necklace.

I use cans tonight instead of turtle shells, which John's father says
could be filled with ghosts.
I wonder what the cans held before—tomato soup,
green beans, peaches, hominy, pickled beets?

John helps me lace the cans so they'll stay on my shins.
Then I'm ready.
My feet sweep/sweep/sweep/
lift/lift/lift. I concentrate to keep the rhythm
because it's been such a long time.

But the cans slip, begin to cut. I study feet ahead of me, who
move with strength, with certainty. Whose cans stay on their
shins, where they belong.
I try to concentrate on the burning wood, the hot sparks,
try to be tougher.
Finally I step out. John sees the shakers
down on my feet. I feel their heaviness.

He ties them tighter, tighter but they slip
over and over as if they really want to touch
this ground, full of rock and water and the shells of our ancestors
where it is always night and somewhere else
spirits like us form a great water serpent
and, no matter what, never stop dancing.

The Eye Clinic

We wait together at the IHS eye clinic.
First, we speak of the cool day,
then you tell me about
your declining eyesight
with a self-deprecating laugh.
I'm blind in my left eye, you say.
I've had cataract surgery
on the other—it took months
for my friends to convince me.
I was so scared to have the doctors
touch my good eye.

But it turned out all right.

My eight-year-old grandson
took real good care of me—
he'd fry me an egg and bring
me coffee every morning.

I could finally see.

You rest your hand on the walker,
your smile never fading as you
look at me through large
bifocals—your eyes full moons split
between heaven and earth.
I smile, too. We sit for a while
in compatible silence until Joe appears
to call you back for your exam.
He speaks to you in Keresan, then says,

Let's take your horse this way,

as you get up and pivot
your walker one way, then another
to ease your journey, straight
and dignified, through the narrow
doorway of the physical.

Post-Op

I know my father's recovery is real
not when he is checked
out of the hospital
but when he plays his vintage records.
Harry Belafonte, Herb Alpert
and The Tijuana Brass.
He likes to play them loud, too,
so there is first
a static *connect*
between needle and vinyl
before the house fills
with trumpet,
Calypso declarations to Angelina
over four decades ago.
Dad sits right there in front
of it all as if he is waiting to catch the trumpet's
notes (and defy all laws of nature) by shaping music
into something tangible with his own hands.

In the Waiting Room

Three of us wait in the
government clinic room.
By the door, a man wears a straw hat
with an eagle feather.
His face is patient, somber.
He measures his words
like pouring molasses.
The other, across the room,
is his opposite.
His words are a rapid, nervous stream
punctuated by a stony riverbed.

Together, they shift from speaking
of daily life to The Bottle that has
divided their lives like tributaries.

The somber man said he gave it to Jesus.
*I couldn't handle it anymore. I gave it to Him
and He took it away from me ten years ago.*

The other man shakes his head in disbelief.
*I can't whip it. I wish I could give it to Him
but it's always there. And my wife left me
last week. She just left.*

His words run into this finality and drop off,
one by one, into the air where they wait
until he can take them in again.

If she'd only come back, I know it'd be different this time.

Todd

It is the day of your discharge and
you are busy stripping institution sheets
from the long hospital twin bed.
I walk by and see you with one hand
on your walker, balancing yourself
like a sailboat steadied by its keel.

For now, you're not a frightened swimmer
in your delusions, and you leave your room
with your clear patient belongings bag
tied to the front of your walker.
It shows your personal effects
like stomach contents.
There is even your Easter basket,
which many patients threw away days ago.
You still have your yellow and green
plastic grass and now-empty eggs.
In your basket, too, you have your
signed discharge instructions, your prescriptions,
and directions to the sample clinic rolled
into one like a cardboard megaphone.

When I look at you, read the psychiatrist's
assessment of your life, of your schizophrenia,
it's hard to believe we are almost the same age.

First Time

Mother never wanted anyone to touch
her feet, to massage and polish them,
to paint them. She thought it would
be demeaning for another.
I only got a manicure for my wedding day—
the color was Windsor.
Now, in her seventy-first year, she finally gives in
to a man named Nhom who undertakes his task
with diligence and somber focus. He whisks years
off her feet with a blade, sloughs them with grainy
cream until they glow like anything new to this world.
Are you from China? my mother asks.
No, Vietnam.
Where is your family? Are they with you?
He shakes his head, extends his hands to hold
an invisible machine gun, finger pulling the trigger.

Bang!   *Bang!*
   Bang!   *Bang!*

1 9 7 5.

He draws this date out slowly
like a magician pulling a red silk scarf like pain
from his chest.

I'm only one left.

This changes the moment. There is a great silence.
Nhom, for a few seconds, looks as if he might cry,
though we all know his stoicism will not allow it.
The reply, *I'm so sorry*, from my mother floats away.
Whereas bullets, much heavier, always seek a target
before they fall, then burn impressions in the ground
to leave no doubt of killing.

Los Alamos

Up in Los Alamos

the sky gathers
storm clouds like a sheepherder
in Navajo country.
When all necessary elements are in place,
they band together,
gather energy, then wait in stillness
of anticipation.

Inside the Blue Window Bistro, diners
admire the bright decor and the patio—a jungle
of flowers beaded by drizzle.
There is little talk of the anniversary of
the bomb on Hiroshima sixty long years ago.
Rather, it is a happy and busy place here.
Regulars laugh, drink French-pressed coffee.

Then a small group enters, their silence out of place here.
A Japanese woman in a red kimono leads them
through an open door to the patio garden.
The rain has stopped. Its brief visit to the desert
is done. The clouds break and go their own way.
No one really notices the changing weather,
just like we don't notice the quiet gathering.

Except they all carry a single sunflower.

Mecca from Our Garage

The Muslims were employed
for odd jobs—to help before—but not after.
Still, I never noticed them much,
except for their efficiency and rapid
Arabic, sounding so strange
near the Mississippi Delta.

They were always together, all three,
never entering a patio gate without invitation.
Most people didn't want them around
even for an honest day's work.
My dad, however, trusted their diligence
and sought them out to divert rainwater
from the flower bed
of soaked petunias and marigolds
in that wet and humid August.

Then one afternoon, home from the movies,
that's when we found them—right in our
garage, kneeling toward Mecca
at the corner of Park and Colonial, praying
on mats. Even when our automatic garage door
growled open, they did not seem startled,
unlike us.
Embarrassed, we backed
the great white nose of our Chrysler
out of their way
and drove around the block.
When we returned, they were finished,
on their way.

Even after seeing them, right there,
facing Mecca in our garage,
I almost did not believe it.
Our garage, full of things
not good enough for the house,
our purgatory,
was made sacred in that moment,
and fitting to lift prayers to Allah.

The Empty Hives

My mother worries over the nightly news. It reports, sandwiched
between the daily murder and seven-day forecast, an unexplained absence of bees.
They are no longer where they once were.

The ghost hives, quiet as a lone cymbal, cannot tell us.

Few shells are found to count. Their fragile wings are
not strewn in any one place like corpses in a war zone.

How will we record these casualties
for our statistics, our cable news conglomerates?

There is no drone to follow.

Where has the Queen taken her following?
So far, even the most advanced technology cannot show us the way,

cannot tell us why.

Black Bear

Officials report
it likely came from the forest
to the city limits
of Muskogee—near the Albertsons
parking lot and Taco Bell—to seek
new territory.

(Though the black bear has no words to tell us.)

The article related tranquilizer darts
weren't successful
and the police had chased him for
at least three hours.
Something had to be done
for the sake of
the children, the fathers and mothers
retrieving *The Muskogee Daily Phoenix* or the
Tulsa World from their driveways,
balancing coffee while opening doors
to their Toyotas or Chevys.

There is a photo of the bear in the tree before
it was shot by the wildlife department—its long
graceful nose, its rounded ears and eyes
disappearing into its black coat—
that is all.
His face is encircled by thick leaves, as if he is part of a holiday wreath.

Like a birth announcement, the article concludes
the bear weighed approximately 150 lbs.,
which is within
normal range for its species.

The black bear must have left our earth at daybreak, when
night sky and its net of stars packed up until tomorrow,
and the sun broke over the power plant on the Arkansas River.
Did his heart wait in its shell
until it could find a place amid the constellations?

Cardinals

In the bleak of a cloudy winter morning, we
spot him on the redwood deck.
He is so still in his red brilliance.
He must know who he is.
Nearby, we see his smaller brown companion.

We return to our toast and bacon.
Uncle Richard is not with us—the one who
loves cardinals the most. He is in Germany now,
near some military base, finessing his clients

with his charm and cans of Spam, corned beef hash,
and plastic bottles of Breck Shampoo, Lavoris, Oil of Olay.
He wears a conservative suit or a golf shirt with
matching slacks. He is on the fast-track,
his company's ace in the hole and a mixed-blood Indian
to boot, even though Uncle Richard never carried
his Indian card like the rest of us.

I wonder what Richard is doing now?
Aunt Julie remarks as she carves a cantaloupe
into slivers of the moon and neatly places
them on pale green stoneware.

Then she pours a tall orange juice and reaches
under the cabinet, the one I wasn't allowed in,
for something clear from a glass bottle that
reads *Vodka* in fancy red letters.

Just an inch or two of *Vodka* lingers on top
like a gasoline rainbow
before she takes a long sip.
Cardinals mate for life
she reports as she looks out to see if he's still
on the patio. The rest of us say nothing, avert
our eyes to our toast and bacon.
She returns to the stove,
as if she could float, and slides an egg,
sunny-side up, on my toast that is almost
perfectly centered in spite of everything.

Tiger Mountain

John's father, who is Muscogee and blind, begins
    to fall silent
when we are in the shadow
of Tiger Mountain.

He says he can discern
when we approach it
and when it becomes
    more distant.

    Tiger Mountain is full of snakes and ghosts, he reports.

I wonder if Tiger Mountain's dense forests
hold night like mercury in a thermometer
that breaks in the morning sun
and tiny poisonous globes scatter
into corners of groundcover, hide beneath decaying leaves,
and transform into silvery diamondbacks.

Trespassing

Warning signs dot edges of woods, rocky coasts and tell us **NO**
with letters in red, black, reflective silver and gold.
They are nailed on fences, hang from ropes, or planted
in the ground—something that will never grow.

My mother used to pull them like a spoiled root vegetable
from their staked claim of land and use them for kindling
between logs to make the fire burn longer and hotter.

The next morning, only ashes and maybe an orange
ember or two remain to be soaked with water and gathered
up with a shovel and thrown back to the earth we only think is our own.

Ice Fishing

My mother tells
of 1960s metal behemoths—
Thunderbirds, Chevys, Fords—
gliding over the Damariscotta River
as if they were little girls on skates—
the ice so thick no one had any fear
of falling through.

They'd park—trusting
the car would stay in park—
beside their ice shanty,
in hopes of catching smelt
that cook up good in a frying pan.
Some would wait for luck
as long as they could stand it—the smell
of rotting bait stronger by the kerosene heater.

They'd wait in the tremendous
snow and pine silence
of rural Maine standing on the center of the Damariscotta
River as if it were an everyday occurrence.

They'd stand on the ice sheet separating
incompatible air and water—
linked by a transparent
fishing line, held in the hands of someone waiting
for the smelt to bite, holding out
just a little longer before
packing up to finally go home on a starlight
path, ready for tomorrow.

Indian in the Majors

I find myself pulling for the Yankees—a new experience—
I blame this on Joba Chamberlain—the broad-shouldered Winnebago
on the pitcher's mound.
He appears to carry the weight of the
need to win
in its fullest sense but radiates no nervous
energy.
He does not chew gum, as if he's trying to harness
power for the machine, a great grist mill
that is his pitching arm.

I watch how he shines
in his pinstripes,
a Bengal tiger stalking prey
in the late summer night.

With each strike he throws,
he controls
in his great silence
and keeps chaos from breaking out
in New York City.

Cold Morning in Bangor

I am told this is true and that the sky looked like snow in the morning—
the sharpness in the air, the gray celestial paths. I am told she was lying on
the ground. Just minutes ago she was talking on the phone to her neighbor
reporting she thought they'd get snow too and her husband had brought her
yellow chrysanthemums from the grocery last night. It had been a long time.
They smelled so fresh—made June seem closer.

Then she was lying on the ground, the laundry basket on its side like a helpless
beetle. The laundry scattered in bits of dirt except for his blue shirt and a white
bath towel she had just hung on the line. Wooden pins were everywhere. Even
though she faced the clouds, she couldn't see them through the clearing fog. Her
hands, clad in white mittens, weren't as cold. The pounding steps of deer hunters
screaming running toward her from the fringe of the woods became more faint.

Pemaquid Point

When the harbor's damp heat
was too much, or we grew tired of waiting
for fog to lift, Dad drove us
to Pemaquid Point lighthouse.
We'd run up and down
rocks like a staircase
of pyramids.
Dad always reminded me
to avoid green, mossy
rocks, knowing I always
liked to get my feet wet
in the salt water, looking
for tidal pools. When I got
too close, I'd feel my mother's
eyes first, behind her giant
black sunglasses, warning
me of how people had been swept away
by a rogue wave that rose up like a
bee from a morning glory.
Of the ocean my mother says
Never let its beauty fool you.

Conjuring Home

I want to wake up to hear the first lonely drone of foghorns
resonate from Ram Island lighthouse who call and call
to vessels on Maine's Atlantic in the darkest dark.

I want to wake up to smell the last smoldering embers from the fire
and musty fishing nets on the back kitchen wall.

I want to wake up and know the tangle of blackberry bushes
are still behind the cottage
and marshmallows will be in the bread box to toss to raccoons at one a.m.

Only now, I imagine the faithful beam of light from Ram Island,
circling, circling, circling,
telling boats it is time to *go home, go home, go home,*
go back to where you should be.

Salmon Run

Leap through the current!
    wait for instinct
to whisper
where they hatched
    where to go now . . .
Those salmon!
Do they realize they are

    red pollen flying?

Red pollen raising their noses
    toward the sky.

At night, the salmon are known
    to eat the stars,
let their silver light increase
    their pinkness

as they take the stars
    beneath the white water.

Those stars always go, silently, like a translucent
    fishing line following its hooked prey.

Except it is different this time.

Then those salmon spit their stars
    into the nighttime
where they reorganize,

reconfigure to form
their usual constellations and galaxies

as if they never
    tasted the saltless river,
    or heard the muffled roar of current meeting stone.